Virtual EI

HBR EMOTIONAL INTELLIGENCE SERIES

HBR Emotional Intelligence Series

How to be human at work

The HBR Emotional Intelligence Series features smart, essential reading on the human side of professional life from the pages of *Harvard Business Review*.

Authentic Leadership	*Mindful Listening*
Confidence	*Mindfulness*
Dealing with Difficult People	*Power and Impact*
Empathy	*Purpose, Meaning, and Passion*
Focus	*Resilience*
Happiness	*Self-Awareness*
Influence and Persuasion	*Virtual EI*
Leadership Presence	

Other books on emotional intelligence from *Harvard Business Review*:

HBR Everyday Emotional Intelligence

HBR Guide to Emotional Intelligence

HBR's 10 Must Reads on Emotional Intelligence

Virtual EI

HBR EMOTIONAL INTELLIGENCE SERIES

Harvard Business Review Press

Boston, Massachusetts

Library of Congress Cataloging-in-Publication Data

Title: Virtual EI.
Other titles: Virtual emotional intelligence | HBR emotional intelligence series.
Description: Boston, Massachusetts : Harvard Business Review Press, 2022. | Series: HBR emotional intelligence series | Includes index.
Identifiers: LCCN 2021058592 (print) | LCCN 2021058593 (ebook) | ISBN 9781647823290 (paperback) | ISBN 9781647823306 (epub)
Subjects: LCSH: Emotional intelligence. | Virtual work. | Telecommuting. | Work environment--Psychological aspects. | Virtual work teams.
Classification: LCC BF576 .V57 2022 (print) | LCC BF576 (ebook) | DDC 152.4—dc23/eng/20211217
LC record available at https://lccn.loc.gov/2021058592
LC ebook record available at https://lccn.loc.gov/2021058593

ISBN: 978-1-64782-329-0
eISBN: 978-1-64782-330-6

The paper used in this publication meets the requirements of the American National Standard for Permanence of Paper for Publications and Documents in Libraries and Archives Z39.48-1992.

Contents

Contents

Contents

Virtual EI

HBR EMOTIONAL INTELLIGENCE SERIES

1

WFH Is Corroding Our Trust in Each Other

By Mark Mortensen and Heidi K. Gardner

Predictability is the foundation of trust. We're willing to be vulnerable—to expose ourselves to potential risk—when we have reason to believe that someone will not take advantage of us or disappoint us. This comes only when we think we can anticipate how others will behave. One of us, Heidi K. Gardner, researched more than 3,000 senior knowledge workers and identified two distinct kinds of trust that are essential for people to work together effectively. First, they need to believe that others will deliver and that the work will be high quality (competence trust). Second, they need to believe that others have good intentions and high integrity (interpersonal trust). To trust colleagues in both of these ways, people need clear and easily discernible signals about them—what they're doing (actions), why they're doing it (motivations), and whether they'll continue to do it (reliability).

Over the past two decades, the moves toward remote working and dynamically shifting teams have made this information harder to come by. Less face-to-face time means that we have less opportunity to observe, for example, that a teammate consistently brings along prepared notes and diagrams to enhance the conversation. We also have fewer shared sidebar conversations that build rapport and interpersonal trust, and we lack situational cues—like the leftover pizza boxes as evidence colleagues pulled an all-nighter—to understand others' efforts and outputs. This makes it difficult to establish trust in others because we don't have the data we need to know what they'll do. It also eliminates the steady stream of reinforcing information that helps us maintain existing trust. The isolation of remote working may be tied to lower trust for another reason: We unconsciously interpret a lack of physical contact as a signal of untrustworthiness.[1]

In virtual work, misunderstandings and miscommunications abound.[2] We therefore face a perfect storm of less information on which to establish trust, less reinforcing information to maintain it, and more "trust infractions" to break it. Once trust is lost, it's very hard to regain.[3] There are a few steps leaders should take to bring trust back to their and their employees' relationships.

Understanding the Science of Trust

An increasingly common approach to dealing with decreased trust is to counter it with increased monitoring.[4] Whether done through technology (for example, keystroke capture) or process (for example, daily check-ins), monitoring is usually counterproductive.

Monitoring fails because it tries to solve the wrong part of the trust equation—it's about managers trying to eliminate the space for vulnerability. The better approach is to leave the space alone but reduce the likelihood that someone will take advantage of it (and you). This doesn't mean trusting blindly, but rather relying on the science of trust to build it in the least risky way possible.

Recognize and leverage reciprocal trust. So often, when we talk about trust, we focus on how we develop it in other people. This misses the fact that trust is bidirectional and reciprocal—research shows that the more you trust someone and act accordingly, the more likely they are to trust you in return. Importantly, these do not operate independently. This means that in order to increase trust within your network, you need to shift your focus to signaling your own trustworthiness. Increasing others' trust in you reduces uncertainty by creating a more stable and certain environment. Thinking in more Machiavellian terms, it also provides reciprocal leverage—the more trust they place in you, the less likely they will be to betray your trust (think mutually assured destruction as the underpinning of the entire Cold War). This is not setting yourself up to be taken advantage of; this is a strategic move that de-risks trust building. And remember that which signals you send is one of the few things you do have control over.

Build a trust staircase. Across substantial research on change (behavior change, culture change, you name it), one message comes through clearly: The best way to create lasting change is through repeated, small, reinforcing steps. Building trust is no exception—it requires evidence and reinforcement. Another way to increase the trust others place in you is to audition for it by finding opportunities to work together on a low-risk task, which gives you a chance to demonstrate your competence and integrity. For example, offer to jointly organize a lunch-and-learn series, where people (not just you) can showcase their abilities. Look for situations that require minimal investments and for which the opportunity and failure costs are low. Demonstrate your own trustworthiness within that context and then, over time, build up to larger and more significant demonstrations to reinforce the trust you're establishing.

Engage in status quo communication. Leaders know how important it is to communicate when things change. However, when things are in a constant state of flux, leaders also need to communicate about things that *aren't* changing. Given that trust depends so heavily on predictability, leaders must recognize the critical importance of helping employees understand what they *can* count on. Doing so reduces uncertainty and creates a needed sense of stability.

Assume one-size-fits-none trusting. Trust building, maintenance, and recovery work differently for different types of people, who fall into two broad categories: automatic trusters and evidence-based trusters.

- Automatic trusters approach a new relationship with at least some level of trust as the default, initially trusting the other party unless something happens to break that trust. This isn't blind trust, but rather an inclination to give the benefit of the doubt. They're minimally affected by fewer trust-building cues, and trust infractions trigger a challenge to their self-image, provoking a more severe and long-lasting backlash.

- Evidence-based trusters approach a new relationship with distrust as the default, not exposing themselves to risk until the other party has proven their trustworthiness. The lack of evidence characteristic of remote work makes it significantly more difficult to establish trust in virtual environments. Once trust is established (based on accumulated evidence), only major infractions are likely to significantly counter or undo that evidence.

A critical first step is to not assume that others build trust as you do. With that in mind, you must do the homework required to know both your own and your counterpart's approaches to trusting and put in the effort to adapt accordingly. If you're an automatic truster and your counterpart is more evidence-based, you need to slow down your expectations and focus on providing that person with ongoing, repeated evidence of your predictability and trustworthiness. If you're building the evidence for your trust case and your counterpart is trusting you on arrival, it's critical that you keep an eye out for your own behaviors that may signal an infraction for them.

To maintain morale and avoid negative outcomes like increased attrition in a remote and hybrid workforce, leaders must take steps to establish (or reestablish) trust among their employees.

MARK MORTENSEN is an associate professor of organizational behavior at INSEAD. He researches, teaches, and consults on issues of collaboration, organizational design and new ways of working, and leadership.

HEIDI K. GARDNER is a distinguished fellow at Harvard Law School and a faculty chair in the school's executive education programs. She is also a cofounder of Gardner & Co. and the author of *Smart Collaboration: How Professionals and Their Firms Succeed by Breaking Down Silos.*

Notes

1. Robert Kurzban, "The Social Psychophysics of Cooperation: Nonverbal Communication in a Public Goods Game," *Journal of Nonverbal Behavior* 25 (2001): 241–259, https://doi.org/10.1023/A:1012563421824.

2. Eric M. Stark and Paul E. Bierly III, "An Analysis of Predictors of Team Satisfaction in Product Development Teams with Differing Levels of Virtualness," *R&D Management* 39, no. 5 (2009): 461–472, https://doi .org/10.1111/j.1467-9310.2009.00571.x.
3. Sandra L. Robinson, Matthew S. Kraatz, and Denise M. Rousseau, "Changing Obligations and the Psychological Contract: A Longitudinal Study," *Academy of Management Journal* 37, no. 1 (1994): 137–152, https://doi .org/10.2307/256773.
4. Alex Hern, "Shirking from Home? Staff Feel the Heat as Bosses Ramp Up Remote Surveillance," *The Guardian*, September 27, 2020, https://www.theguardian.com/ world/2020/sep/27/shirking-from-home-staff-feel-the -heat-as-bosses-ramp-up-remote-surveillance.

Adapted from content posted on hbr.org,
February 10, 2021 (product #H066NN).

2

What Psychological Safety Looks Like in a Hybrid Workplace

By Amy C. Edmondson and Mark Mortensen

Since the pandemic changed the landscape of work, much attention has been given to the more visible aspects of WFH, including the challenges of managing people from a distance (including reduced trust and new power dynamics). But a far less visible factor may dramatically influence the effectiveness of hybrid workplaces. Sorting out new forms of work arrangements, and attending to employees' inevitable anxieties about those arrangements, requires managers to rethink and expand one of the strongest proven predictors of team effectiveness: psychological safety.

How New Forms of Work Affect Psychological Safety

Psychological safety—the belief that one can speak up without risk of punishment or humiliation—has been well established as a critical driver of high-quality decision making, healthy group dynamics and inter-personal relationships, greater innovation, and more-effective execution in organizations. Simple as it may be to understand, Amy's work has shown how hard it is to establish and maintain psychological safety even in the most straightforward, factual, and critical contexts—for example, ensuring that operating room staff speak up to avoid a wrong-side surgery, or that a CEO is corrected before sharing inaccurate data in a public meeting (both are real-life psychological safety failure examples reported in interviews). Unfortunately, WFH and hybrid working make psychological safety anything but straightforward.

When it comes to psychological safety, managers have traditionally focused on enabling candor and dissent with respect to work content. The problem is, with the blurring of the boundary between work and life, managers must make staffing, scheduling, and coordination decisions that take into account employees' personal circumstances—a categorically different domain.

For one employee, the decision of when to work from home may be driven by a need to spend time with a widowed parent or to help a child struggling at school. For another, it may be influenced by un-disclosed health issues (something Covid-19 brought into stark relief) or a nonwork passion, as was the case with a young professional who trained as an Olympic-level athlete on the side. It's worth noting that we've both heard from employees who feel mar-ginalized, penalized, or excluded from this dialogue around work-life balance because they're single or have no children, often being told they're lucky they don't have to deal with those challenges. Having psychologically safe discussions around work-life balance issues is challenging because these topics are more likely to touch on deep-seated aspects of employees' identity, values, and choices. This makes them both more personal and riskier from legal and ethical standpoints with respect to bias.

We Can't Just Keep Doing What We're Doing

In the past, we've approached "work" and "nonwork" discussions as separable, allowing managers to keep the latter off the table. During the pandemic, however, many managers found that previously off-limits topics like childcare, health-risk comfort levels, or challenges faced by spouses or other family members are increasingly required for joint (manager and employee) decisions about how to structure and schedule hybrid work.

While it may be tempting to think we can re-separate the two when some or most employees return to the office, the shift to a higher proportion of WFH means that's neither a realistic nor a sustainable long-term solution. Organizations that don't update their approach will find themselves trying to optimize extremely complicated scheduling and coordination challenges with incomplete—if not incorrect—information. Keep in mind that hybrid working arrangements present a parallel increase in managerial complexity; managers face the same workflow coordination challenges they've managed in the past, with the added challenge of coordinating among people who can't be counted on to be present at predictable times.

Strategies for Managers

Let's start with the fact that the reasons why managers have avoided seeking personal details remain just as relevant and critical as they've always been. Sharing personal information carries real and significant risks, given legal restrictions related to asking personal questions, the potential for bias, and a desire to respect employee privacy. The solution thus cannot be to demand greater disclosure of personal details. Instead, managers must create an environment that encourages employees to share aspects of their personal situations as relevant to their work scheduling or location and/or to trust employees to make the right choices for themselves and their families, balanced against the needs of their teams. Management's responsibility is to expand the domain of which work-life issues are safe to raise. Psychological safety is needed today to enable productive conversations in new, challenging (and potentially fraught) territory.

Obviously, simply saying "just trust me" won't work. Instead, we suggest a series of five steps to create a culture of psychological safety that extends beyond the work content to include broader aspects of employees' experiences.

Step 1: Set the scene

Trite as it sounds, the first step is having a discussion with your team members to help them recognize not only their challenges but yours as well. The objective of this discussion is to share ownership of the problem.

We suggest framing this as a need for the group to problem solve to develop new ways to work effectively. Clarify what's at stake. Employees must understand that getting the work done (for customers, for the mission, for their careers) matters just as much as it always has, but that it won't be done exactly as it was in the past—they'll need to play a (creative and responsible) role in that. As a group, you and your employees must come to recognize that everyone must be clear and transparent about the needs of the work and of the team and jointly own responsibility for succeeding, despite the many hurdles that lie ahead.

Step 2: Lead the way

Words are cheap, and when it comes to psychological safety, there are far too many stories of managers who demand candor of their employees—particularly around mistakes or other potentially embarrassing topics—without demonstrating it themselves or without protecting it when others do share.

The best way to show you're serious is to expose your own vulnerability by sharing your own WFH/hybrid work personal challenges and constraints. Remember, managers have to go first in taking these kinds of risks. Be vulnerable and humble about not having a clear plan and be open about how you're thinking about managing your own challenges. If you're not willing to be candid with your employees, why should you expect them to be candid with you?

Step 3: Take baby steps

Don't expect your employees to share their most personal and risky challenges right away. It takes time to build trust, and even if you have a healthy culture of psychological safety established around work, remember that this is a new domain, and speaking up about buggy code is different from sharing struggles at home.

Start by making small disclosures yourself, and then make sure to welcome others' disclosures to help your employees build confidence that sharing is not penalized.

Step 4: Share positive examples

Don't assume that your employees will immediately have access to all the information you have supporting the benefits of sharing these challenges and needs.

Put your marketing hat on and market psychological safety by sharing your conviction that increased transparency is happening and is helping the team design new arrangements that serve both individual needs and organizational goals. The goal here isn't to share information that was disclosed to you privately but rather to explain that disclosure has allowed you to collaboratively come up with solutions that were better not just for the team but also for the employees. This needs to be done with tact and skill to avoid creating pressure to conform—the goal here is to provide employees with the evidence they need to buy in voluntarily.

Step 5: Be a watchdog

Most people recognize that psychological safety takes time to build, but moments to destroy. The default is for people to hold back, to fail to share even their most relevant thoughts at work if they're not sure they'll be well received. When they do take the risk of speaking up, but get shot down, they—and everyone else—will be less likely to do it the next time.

As a team leader, be vigilant and push back when you notice employees making seemingly innocent comments like "We want to see more of you" or "We could really use you," which may leave employees feeling they're letting their teammates down. This is a really hard thing to do and requires skill. The idea isn't to become thought police or punish those who genuinely do miss their WFH colleagues or need their help, but rather to help employees frame these remarks in a more positive and understanding way— for example, "We miss your thoughtful perspective, and understand you face constraints. Let us know if there is any way we can help . . ." Be open about your intentions to be inclusive and helpful so that people don't see requests for their presence as a rebuke. At the same time, be ready to firmly censure those who inappropriately take advantage of shared personal information.

It's important to view (and discuss) these conversations as a work in progress. As with all group dynamics, they're emergent processes that develop and shift over time. This is a first step; the journey ahead comes without a road map and will have to be navigated iteratively. You may overstep and need to correct, but it's better to err on the side of trying and testing the waters than assuming topics are off-limits. View this as a learning or problem-solving undertaking that may never reach a steady state. The more you maintain that perspective—rather than declaring victory and moving on—the more successful you and your team will be at developing and maintaining true, expanded psychological safety.

AMY C. EDMONDSON is the Novartis Professor of Leadership and Management at Harvard Business School. She is the author of *The Fearless Organization: Creating Psychological Safety in the Workplace for Learning, Innovation, and Growth.*

MARK MORTENSEN is an associate professor of organizational behavior at INSEAD. He researches, teaches, and consults on issues of collaboration, organizational design and new ways of working, and leadership.

Adapted from content posted on hbr.org,
April 19, 2021 (product #H06AWX).

3

Write Down Your Team's Unwritten Rules

By Liz Fosslien and Mollie West Duffy

very workplace has unwritten rules. If you're on a video call with 20 of your colleagues, is it okay to turn off your camera? When you email your boss, do you include a bunch of emojis?

During stressful times (such as a global pandemic), it's good practice to write down the unstated cultural and emotional norms that exist within your team or company. They might have changed during Covid-19, or perhaps they've never been explicit to everyone. You might know that it's okay to take a walk in the middle of the day to clear your head, but it might not be obvious to your colleagues, especially if they're new hires. These seemingly small uncertainties ("Can

I step outside to take a short break?") can become major stressors. Combating them is crucial to helping everyone on your team feel secure and supported.

In our book *No Hard Feelings*, one of our most popular suggestions is to write an "It's okay to . . ." list. We heard about the idea from the writer Giles Turnbull, who wanted to emphasize to new employees at the U.K. Government Digital Service that it was always okay to do things like ask for help, make mistakes, and have off days. He drafted a list, asked his colleagues to add other ideas, and then designed posters that he hung all over his office. His final list included things like "It's okay to . . .":

- Say you don't understand

- Not know everything

- Have quiet days

- Ask why, and why not

- Ask management to fix it

Lists like these surface permissions that already exist within workplace cultures, but that not everyone is aware of or that people often need reminding of. Matt Reiter, director at World 50, a private community for C-suite executives, created a list with his team. "It was clear things had changed since my team started working from home [during the pandemic], but no one had acknowledged them," he said. "There are things I know it's okay to do, but that knowledge comes from my seniority and time at the company. If it's okay for me to take a mental health day, it's okay for you as well."

Even the simplest reminders can lead people to change their behavior. Researchers at Google sent new hires an email reminding them that top performers at the organization regularly "ask questions, lots of questions!" and "actively solicit feedback—don't wait for it." Just listing that helped new hires practice and develop those skills, increasing their productivity by 2%, an increase of about $400 million per year.

The pandemic demonstrated we need to be ready to adapt to an ever-changing world. We encourage teams to document their unofficial rules by creating "It's okay to . . ." lists. You might include things like "It's okay to . . .":

- Turn off your video if you need a break during longer calls

- Shift your hours earlier or later to take care of family commitments

- Have a child or pet pop into the video screen

- Block off no-meeting time on your calendar for focused work

- Request a voice rather than video call

We've also heard of a few organizations that create event-related specific lists (such as around the time of a critical election) that include items like "It's okay to . . ." form discussion support groups, take the day off to vote, or ask for help prioritizing work if you feel overwhelmed.

Here are a few areas to consider when putting together a list for your team or organization:

Digital communication norms

Hopping on back-to-back video calls is draining, so be explicit about when people can turn off their cameras and when they should plan to have them on. For example, in small groups where you're doing a lot of discussion or collaboration, it may be important to have everyone visible. But at many workplaces, video calls have become the default, even for meetings when a phone call or no-video call would suffice. So decide the appropriate channel for your meeting, and communicate it clearly. Or maybe your team agrees that everyone should turn on video for the first 10 minutes of a call to establish a connection, and then make it okay to turn it off for the remainder of the meeting.

We also recommend thinking through and coming to agreement on whether it's okay to . . . have kids pop up, answer the door if a package arrives, or get up during a longer meeting to stretch or get a drink. These can all alleviate anxiety and level the playing field among employees.

Emotional support

In tough and uncertain times, we're not always going to perform at our best. Consider making it okay to have an off day or to take a break in the afternoon. Beth Heltebridle, a branch librarian at the Frederick County Library in Maryland, shared with us that she made a list with her branch leadership team during their library closure due to Covid. Beth told us, "We shared our list out to build morale in these trying times and have been sending it to new hires now that we are onboarding again. One of the hardest things is that our days look so different, and we miss interactions with other team members. Some of these 'unsaid rules' may be missed in our current situation, so we wanted to be sure to state them to new members and remind the rest of the team that our culture remains unchanged."

The library's list includes items such as it's okay to . . . not check your email during off-hours, say yes when someone offers to grab you a coffee, ask for patience, and make space to concentrate.

Psychological safety

New hires are the most likely employees to lack a sense of belonging and psychological safety. That's why it's especially important to emphasize to new hires that it's okay to ask lots of questions and not feel like you know everything a week into starting your new job. Being remote makes it harder to get answers to small questions. And given the economic climate, many people feel lucky to even have a job or are terrified of losing theirs, which may make people feel especially hesitant to reach out for fear of coming across as needy, slow, or annoying.

But if people aren't asking questions, either they aren't doing their job as well as they could be, or they're spending precious brainpower on worrying about how they're being perceived. These lists give permission for everyone to ask questions. Include specifics, like it's okay to . . . ask questions, even if you think they're silly, or ask clarifying questions about questions you've already asked.

Work styles

We often work with people who have very different work styles, from extreme extroverts to cautious decision makers to assertive debaters. Often the work styles that get most normalized at an organization are those of the people in power or in the majority. For example, if most leaders are extroverts, an organization may default to large meetings and collaborative sessions. You could use an "it's okay to . . ." list to help people with different work styles feel more comfortable, emphasizing that they don't have to adapt to belong.

You could make it okay for introverts to rely on the chat function in a video call rather than unmuting themselves and speaking, or to ask for more time when making an important decision. Briley Noel Hutchison, a program manager at Girl Scouts–Diamonds of Arkansas, Oklahoma, and Texas, told us that her program team made it okay to be direct, to have space for silence, and to follow up with people to help projects stay on track.

As an added bonus, these lists can turn into recruiting tools. Giles Turnbull told us, "Several people said they'd applied for jobs at the Government Digital Service as a direct result of seeing the blog post about the posters or of seeing images of them on social media. One photo of one poster became a powerful recruitment asset."

The act of making a list is a simple exercise that has positive benefits for new, tenured, and future employees—and allows you to reinforce your culture even when the nature of work changes.

LIZ FOSSLIEN is the head of content at Humu, a company that makes it easy for teams to improve, every single week. She has designed and led sessions related to emotions at work for audiences including TED, LinkedIn, Google, Viacom, and Spotify. Liz's writing and illustrations have been featured by *The Economist*, Freakonomics, and NPR.

MOLLIE WEST DUFFY is an organizational development expert and consultant. She was previously an organizational design lead at global innovation firm IDEO and a research associate for the dean of Harvard Business School, Nitin Nohria, and renowned strategy professor Michael E. Porter. She's written for *Fast Company, Quartz, Stanford Social Innovation Review, Entrepreneur*, and other digital outlets.

They are the coauthors of *No Hard Feelings: The Secret Power of Embracing Emotions at Work*. Follow them on Twitter or Instagram @lizandmollie.

Adapted from content posted on hbr.org,
October 26, 2020 (product #H05YGL).

4

The Endless Digital Workday

By Arjun Narayan, Rohan Narayana Murty, Rajath B. Das, and Scott Duke Kominers

Companies all over the world are redefining their vision of what it means to be "at work." While digital technologies like email and smartphones have always blurred the distinction between being at work and being out of the office, for many white-collar workers, the pandemic eliminated any separation that might have remained.

To restore balance and sustain productivity, leaders need to reckon with exactly what happened to their employees' work lives. Unlike with prior digital work technologies, which were typically adopted first either by the busiest executives (top-down) or by employees in field support, sales, or remote locations (outside-in), Covid-19 forced many office teams into working *solely* atop digital technologies all the time. For the average worker and frontline manager who were used to working in a standard physical location during "regular hours"—usually 9 a.m. to 5 p.m.—the change was abrupt and disorienting, necessitating new plans and expectations. And as hybrid and remote options became mainstream, companies needed to incorporate positive and negative learnings from the pandemic year. The "new normal" demanded new norms for work itself.

One of the basic factors in determining these work norms is the concept of "team overlap," that is, the extent to which the work hours of different team members coincide. In the physical workplace, having regular work hours typically guarantees a high degree of overlap between one team member and the rest of the team. With remote and hybrid work, that level of overlap is not as common.

To understand the patterns and implications of team overlap during remote work, we studied the work behaviors of 187 individuals across six *Fortune* 500 companies that transitioned to remote work in 2020. (These companies were all clients of Soroco, an enterprise software company focused on understanding the "work graph" of how teams interact digitally, where three of the authors work.) The workers in our sample were spread across 22 teams, with an average team size of about 10 members. All of these workers previously had well-defined office locations and office hours; virtually none of them do now.

We found a number of patterns in the teams' work behavior and saw in particular that overlap is important to consider when developing norms for remote and hybrid work. Understanding these trends is essential to figuring how to lead teams as they navigate these modes of working. Managers can use these sorts of analyses in guiding a digital team charter, which can help preserve the flexibility of remote and hybrid work, while counteracting the psychological and practical downsides many workers experienced during the pandemic.

Always On, but Never All Together

Our findings confirm a now-familiar truth: The digital workday never really ends. On average, individual team members are available for work for eight-plus hours in the day—using the conservative measurement of "being available for work" as being on a work computer for 30+ minutes in the hour. On average, teams are on their PCs for 45 minutes each hour, for 6.1 hours of effort over the course of each 24-hour workday (as outlined in figure 1).

The remote workday is divided into two distinct portions: an eight-hour window from 9 to 5 when team members generally work together and a 16-hour window when team members generally work apart. During the first window, team members on average overlap with 50% to 70% of their colleagues and can generally be considered to be working together. During the longer "off hours" window, team members overlap with 10% to 50% of their colleagues and can thus be considered to be working apart.

The graph of this data tells us a few important things.

In the 9 a.m. to 5 p.m. window when there's the highest overlap, there are two peaks, one at 10 a.m. and another at 3 p.m.; outside of this range, there are low ebbs, but no time when everyone is completely off. This insight, in turn, contains four empirical observations that are the proverbial "elephants in the room" that managers must account for in remote and hybrid work: Digital workers are *working odd hours alone*; the digital workday is *truly endless*; the digital team is *usually not all together*; and *midday constraints matter* much more during the digital workday.

First, the digital day implies *working odd hours, alone.* The "regular" work hours of 9 to 5 have survived the transition to remote work, but they account for only 60% of the work effort of the team. An average team member on an average team spends

FIGURE 1

When is your team working?

Digital teams work around the clock. While team members regularly spend eight or more hours a day on their work computers, they're not necessarily working at the same time. The teams are never 100% switched off, nor are they 100% switched on.

The remote workday.

Percentage of team members available for work.
On a work computer for 30 or more minutes in the hour

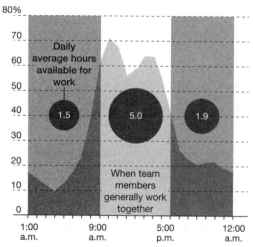

The hourly productivity of these teams does not change significantly over the hours of the workday, even though the mix and number of business processes performed changes.

Average hourly productivity of online team members.
As a multiple of daily average

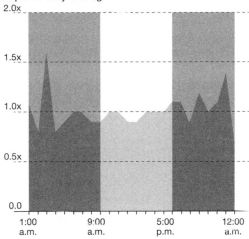

Survey of 187 individuals across six *Fortune* 500 companies who transitioned to remote work In 2020.
Source: Arjun Narayan et al., hbr.org

40% of their work hours essentially working apart from their team members—and outside of regular working hours.

Second, the digital day is truly *endless*. We are all familiar with the phenomenon of emails arriving from team members at all hours of the day—from team members who log on early or burn the midnight oil. What our data shows us is that this is not a scattered or one-off phenomenon. Even at the lowest point in the workday—4 a.m.—on average 10+% of the team is available and putting in 30+ minutes of work in the hour. Given that the team size in the sample is 10.2 individuals, this means that one member of the team is typically online and working, no matter what time of day or night it is.

Third, digital teams are *rarely all together.* In our data set, we saw a few teams that mimicked in-person hours, meaning that 90% of the team was online during traditional work hours. However, this is not the norm. The average overlap measured across all 22 teams in our data set maxes out at approximately 71% during 10 to 11 a.m., and then again at 60% during 3 to 4 p.m. This means, on average, that at least 29% of the team is not online—no matter what hour of the workday it is.

Fourth, *midday constraints matter*. Team overlap drops gradually after 10 a.m. to a trough in the 12 to 1 p.m. slot before recovering gradually again for the 3 p.m. afternoon peak. This slow drop and extended recovery are produced by different members of the team taking breaks at different points in the middle of the workday. There is no longer any social reason for people to take their lunch breaks together, so in the digital world, they lunch on their own time.

All these changes make the digital workday practically and psychologically different from traditional office work.

Does the Work Schedule Actually Matter?

What does all of this mean for productivity?

While our data set does not contain time tracking from before our teams transitioned to remote work, we observed (the second graph) that—on average—there was no correlation between the time of the day and hourly productivity. The 22 teams in our data set performed a total of 39 business processes, and each team member could choose when they performed each task. In effect, *team members naturally scheduled their work so that their hourly productivity was constant.*

Greater or lower team overlap was, however, an important factor for productivity, and by looking at how hourly productivity is related to team overlap, we saw that the business processes performed by our teams fall into three categories, according to whether having other team members online can help, hurt, or have no effect on completing certain tasks.

- *41% of business processes were positively correlated with team overlap.* Having a colleague around to give you that input you needed or to help you clarify how to do your work is often productive. In 16 of the 39 processes that we studied, we saw workers were nearly 25% more productive during 9 to 5 than time elsewhere. Examples of such work include finalizing rates for insurance quotes, creating and approving production plans, and managing changes to the inventory.

- *33% of business processes were neutrally correlated with team overlap.* In 13 of the 39 processes that we studied, productivity did not appear to depend on whether team members were working at the same time—and thus, it didn't seem to matter when in the workday these tasks were completed. Examples of such work include creating purchase orders and monitoring supply-demand status of products and warehouse allocations.

- *26% of business processes were negatively correlated with team overlap.* In 10 of the 39 processes that we studied, team overlap was associated with low productivity—28% lower during regular work hours, compared with times with lower team overlap. Perhaps worryingly, team members often conducted these processes between 9 a.m. and 5 p.m. when there was high overlap. (That said, our data does not allow us to rule out the possibility that some of the negative correlation in this category was driven by team members shifting work on the most difficult parts of tasks to periods of high overlap.) Examples of such work include releasing purchase orders and updating employee details in a database.

Business processes in the first category benefit from team members working together at the same time; those in the second category are particularly good candidates for being conducted remotely in the long run; and those in the third category would benefit from explicit norms allowing team members to work on them remotely without distraction.

Lessons for Managers

Managers must consider how the digital workday might lead team members to push themselves harder or work odd hours. In some cases, team members may need to work for more hours in order to achieve the same outcomes. In other cases, the amount of work time may appear more burdensome when performed alone, at odd hours of the day or night, without much social cohesion and contact.

Teams can address these challenges through a digital team charter, which establishes norms on work hours and team overlap. Some specific areas of focus include:

- *Making time to be together.* You should establish "together hours" where 50+% of the team is expected to be online and working together. In our data set, we saw that teams had on average seven-plus hours in the workday during which more than half the team was consistently online. Those hours are also when you should schedule business processes that benefit from having greater team overlap—as well as making and communicating decisions that affect the entire group. (See "Open Your (Virtual) Door" for another way to be "together.")

- *Not forcing overlap.* You shouldn't be concerned if your team is not overlapping in a contiguous seven-hour block, or if the team is unable to achieve 50+% overlap all the time. (In our data set, we saw team overlap range from four to 10 hours a day.) In every team there are processes that appear to be best performed individually, at times of low overlap.

- *Not micromanaging schedules.* Allow your employees the flexibility to schedule their business processes as per their personal timing preferences. In our data, most team members appeared to naturally conduct their work at the times of the day when those business processes could be most efficiently performed.

- *Letting people log off.* Establish norms for your team members to take the time and space

OPEN YOUR (VIRTUAL) DOOR

Physical distance can lead to psychological distance. It's much easier to check in on colleagues when sharing a physical space. Often, one glance is enough to tell if Sarah over in finance is having a bad day. Office exchanges with colleagues outside immediate working areas or departments have a positive effect on organizational functioning and can impact effective performance.[1] These informal communications contribute to an organization's culture and functionality more than communication tools like email and instant messaging do.[2]

One solution is to open the virtual office door. In the past, an open physical door signaled that it was okay to walk in and speak with your colleague. Without visible cues for how busy a colleague is, people might hesitate to reach out to them. When working remotely, make use of the trusty status bar. A message like "Open for chats!" along with a green status circle gives folks permission to bridge the distance gap. Companies can also develop a sense of place with virtual reality and virtual meeting rooms to create a sense of belonging and sharing. The virtual meeting technology space is burgeoning, giving employers more and more options for how to bring these rooms to life.

Grace Lordan is an associate professor in behavioral science at the London School of Economics and Political Science. She is an expert on the effects of bias, discrimination, and technology changes. Grace is the founder and director of the Inclusion Initiative, a research center at LSE, and the author of *Think Big: Take Small Steps and Build the Career You Want.*

Teresa Almeida is a behavioral science researcher at the Inclusion Initiative.

Lindsay Kohler is an applied behavioral scientist who consults with *Fortune* 500 companies on their employee engagement efforts. She currently contributes to *Forbes* and is a coauthor of *Even Better If: Building Better Businesses, Better Leaders, and Better Selves.*

Excerpted from "5 Practices to Make Your Hybrid Workplace Inclusive," by Grace Lordan, Teresa Almeida, and Lindsay Kohler, on hbr.org, August 17, 2021 (product #H06IRG).

to do focused work. These take two forms: "heads down" time, that is, specific hours in the calendar where no team meetings are to be scheduled and team members are expected not to contact each other unless absolutely necessary, and "do not disturb" flags that individuals can use to signal when they need to focus.

The digital charter you create shouldn't be a static document—you should revisit it regularly (say, at the start of each quarter) as your team gains experience with digital collaboration.

Managers also need to focus on reducing the toil of digital work. This presents serious challenges in a remote/hybrid work context since managers can no longer walk the hallway and build managerial intuition on a *sustained program of toil reduction*. Reducing physical toil requires objective assessment of what the end user is doing at work; how that work is organized into structured versus unstructured processes; and how those processes can be improved through multiple levers such as process improvement, user training, automation, and upgrade of underlying IT applications.

Managers can rebuild their intuition through periodic retrospectives (as part of their digital team charter), via the use of internal or external operations consulting teams, or via the use of new tools that apply computer science to understanding how teams work in a digital environment.

Remote work is here to stay and, with it, new challenges for collaboration and productivity. Our research corroborates prior accounts of the remote workday as being "unending"—with productivity stretched across all hours and periods of employee isolation. At the same time, we found that working alone can sometimes be productive, and in many cases, employees seem to be doing a good job of allocating tasks across different periods of the day.

Our analysis highlights the importance of establishing norms around team overlap and suggests some simple strategies for combating the remote work's practical and psychological downsides. With this sort of research, we can use lessons from the pandemic period to improve business operations—and make them more sustainable for employees in the long run.

ARJUN NARAYAN is chief product officer and cofounder of Soroco. He leads Soroco's efforts in using machine learning to discover and optimize how teams get work done in the enterprise.

ROHAN NARAYANA MURTY is the CTO and founder of Soroco. He leads technology and R&D at Soroco, where he is building the work graph—a new data fabric for understanding how teams get work done in the enterprise.

RAJATH B. DAS is a senior research analyst at Soroco, focusing on analytical insights derived from the work graph—patterns in how teams get work done in the enterprise.

SCOTT DUKE KOMINERS is the MBA Class of 1960 Associate Professor of Business Administration in the Entrepreneurial Management Unit at Harvard Business School and a faculty affiliate of the Harvard Department of Economics. Prior to that, he was a junior fellow at the Harvard Society of Fellows and the inaugural Saieh Family Fellow in Economics at the Becker Friedman Institute.

Notes

1. Pamela Brandes, Ravi Dharwadkar, and Kathleen Wheatley, "Social Exchanges Within Organizations and Work Outcomes: The Importance of Local and Global Relationships," *Group and Organization Management* 29, no. 3 (June 2004): 276–301, https://doi.org/10.1177/1059601103257405.
2. Maya Orbach et al., "Sensing Informal Networks in Organizations," *American Behavioral Scientist* 59, no. 4 (April 2015): 508–524, https://doi.org/10.1177/0002764214556810.

Adapted from content posted on hbr.org,
August 12, 2021 (product #H06HJX).

5

Find Your Focus and Stop Zoning Out in Zoom Meetings

By Sarah Gershman

You join a videoconference call. You're one of nine faces on the screen. About 10 minutes into the call, your mind starts to wander and you realize you have no idea what the last person just said. You pretend to keep listening while also checking your inbox. By the end of the meeting, you've caught up on some email but ultimately feel like it was another waste of time. For many of us right now, this scenario sounds all too familiar.

There is a lot of sound advice about how leaders can run more-effective virtual meetings. While this advice is critical, what is often overlooked is the role that *listeners* play in ensuring a meeting's success.

In 1913, Max Ringelmann, a French architectural engineer, made a discovery that actually explains why virtual meetings are often so unsuccessful. Ringelmann asked a team of people to pull on a rope. He then asked individuals—separately—to pull on the same rope. He noticed that when people worked as individuals, they put more effort into pulling than when they worked as a team. We call this the "Ringelmann effect." The bigger the group, the less responsibility each individual feels to ensure success. If one does not feel critical to a mission's success, it's easy to tune out or put in less effort. No one will notice anyway, right?

In virtual meetings—and especially on conference calls—the Ringelmann effect is magnified. When you're not in the room to help "pull the rope" for a meeting, you might feel less motivated to listen and participate. The less you feel needed, the more distracted you will become, and the less you will give to the meeting. And the less you give, the less fulfilling the experience.

How can you minimize the Ringelmann effect and give more to (and get more from) virtual meetings? It's not through more or louder participation. Rather, the secret to effective participation involves thoughtful and targeted *listening*. Especially in a virtual context, listening needs to be active, participatory, and helpful. Here are five strategies to listen more effectively in your next virtual meeting:

1. Define your value beforehand

Take a few moments before the meeting starts to distill the purpose of the meeting and what your value could be. What is the most critical information you have? What is it you want to contribute? Be ready with those points. If you don't have a critical role to play or don't need to present any information, identify exactly what you hope to learn from the call. Figuring this out ahead of time will help you listen more carefully to what's being said and strengthen a listening muscle for future meetings.

2. Acknowledge previous statements

Participants sometimes jump in to make their point without first listening to or acknowledging what has just been said. In response, people may repeat or re-hash earlier points, as they don't feel heard or understood. All of this slows down the meeting and leads to a disjointed and frustrating conversation. This dynamic is magnified in a virtual meeting, where people often talk over one another. Active listening can help. Before you raise a new topic, reiterate what you just heard or the previous point you plan to riff on—even ask the speaker whether you've characterized their point correctly. Not only does this help the conversation, but it makes it more likely that others will hear what you have to say. People are more likely to listen if they first feel heard.

3. Connect the dots

Leading a virtual meeting is hard. Participants often provide scattershot commentary, and it's tough for a leader to keep the conversation running smoothly. Again, your ability to listen will help. Listen carefully to participants' contributions and then see how you can reflect on what you've heard to help move the conversation forward. For example, let's say over the course of a meeting you notice that several participants mention that a client is frustrated. You might say, "I've heard several people say that the client seems frustrated. I wonder if anyone has any thoughts on why this frustration is happening right now?" Notice that you are not actually giving any new information.

By listening first and then connecting the dots, you can help the other participants understand the larger dynamic and guide the conversation in a productive direction. Effective listening manifests itself when you speak up and reflect on what you've heard.

4. Bring your attention back

Despite your best efforts to listen, it's natural for your mind to wander during the call. It happens to even the best listeners. As with meditation, try to gently note the distracting thought and return your attention to the call. It helps to have a pad of paper next to you. This act of writing down wandering thoughts allows you to put the thought "somewhere" so that you can return to it later, after the meeting has ended. You can also write down any distracting thoughts before the meeting starts, which can help you to be more present and ready to listen.

5. Don't be afraid to ask a question

Sometimes when you get distracted and then return your focus to the meeting, you may find that you are lost, as the conversation has moved in a new direction, and you missed the transition. Give yourself a few minutes to get back on track, and don't be afraid to ask a clarifying question. You might say, "I apologize. I lost track of the conversation for a moment. Would someone please help me understand why we are now focusing on . . ." This may also help others on the call, as it is likely you're not the only one who is confused.

In the isolation of the virtual world, we often feel like we have to fight to be heard, lest our voice get lost in the noise. Once again, listening comes to the rescue. Ironically, one of the best ways to be heard is to be a good listener. Thoughtful, active listening raises your status in the conversation and makes it more likely that others will want to sit up and listen to you. Perhaps most importantly, active, thoughtful listening is a precious gift to your colleagues. It provides meaningful connection during a time and place when people need it most.

SARAH GERSHMAN is the president of Green Room Speakers, a communications firm based in Washington, DC. She is a professor at the McDonough School of Business at Georgetown University, where she teaches public speaking to students from around the globe.

Adapted from "Stop Zoning Out in Zoom Meetings," on hbr.org, May 4, 2020 (product #H05L11).

6

Elevate Your Presence in a Virtual Meeting

By Joel Schwartzberg

Communication practices that work well among colleagues in a conference room don't always translate seamlessly to a computer screen. Elevating both your point and your presence in a virtual or hybrid meeting requires not only engaging in videoconference-friendly tactics but also disabusing yourself of potentially detrimental misconceptions about the medium.

To help keep your impact actual when your presence is virtual, follow these six basic best practices.

1. Focus on your camera, not your colleagues

Every presentation coach will tell you that direct eye contact is a vital way to reinforce your point. In a videoconference, this means looking into the video camera, not at the smiling faces of other participants. Speaking into a cold black circle doesn't feel natural or comfortable—as humans, we're trained to look at the people we're talking to—but it's something successful entertainers and politicians master.

It's challenging to focus on your camera for an entire meeting—especially while others are talking—but you increase the impact of what you're saying when you look deep into the dot.

Practice looking into your camera during videoconferences when you speak, even for brief moments. The more you use it, the more comfortable you'll become with it.

2. Maintain a strong voice

I always counsel my students and clients to use a louder-than-usual voice in video calls because, in addition to being audible, strong voices convey authority, credibility, and confidence. This concept is just as true in virtual settings as it is in actual ones. So even though you're using an external or internal microphone and may be tempted to speak at a conversational volume, maintain a strong, clear voice as if you're in a large conference room.

Using a loud voice will also keep you from mumbling and from speaking too quickly due to the amount of breath required.

3. Frame yourself wisely

Take time before a meeting to pick your location and put your head fully in the frame to ensure you're putting your best face forward. Proximity plays a big part in how audiences perceive you as a communicator. The farther away or more obscured you appear, the less engaging you will be. In a videoconference, your head and the top of your shoulders should dominate the screen. If your head is cut off at the top or bottom, you're too close. If your entire torso is in view, you're too far away.

Also be mindful of your background. Cluttered rooms make communicators seem disorganized. Distracting elements draw attention away from you. Find an environment where the background is simple and professional (or take advantage of an integrated background tool).

4. Be present and mindful

Even if you don't need to be fully engaged in a meeting, your professional reputation can suffer if it looks like you're not paying attention. It's easy to forget you're being watched in a videoconference where you're muted. You may be tempted to check your email or attend to other work, but multitasking is perilous; you don't want to be caught unprepared if someone suddenly asks you a question.

Because you're less aware of social cues in a virtual meeting, it's also important to be mindful of how long and how often you speak, if you interrupt other people, and if you make a comment that might offend someone present but out of sight.

So close those other windows, turn your phone upside down, wait a beat before jumping in if you've already spoken, and remember that you're always "on camera."

5. Don't become a distraction

Talking while muted, annoying ambient noise, and the interference of pets and children are all common pitfalls of virtual meetings, and they can quickly sabotage your point. You want to be remembered for what you did right, not for what went wrong, so take steps to control your virtual and physical environments.

Train yourself to stay on mute whenever you're not speaking and unmute yourself only when you do speak. Staying on mute shuts out sudden noises as well as routine noises you may not be aware of, like the ticking of a wall clock, the clickety-clack of your typing, or even your own breathing.

And turn off your camera when you're doing something visually distracting as well, such as moving to another room or eating.

6. Use the chat window

The chat window in virtual meetings is a unique opportunity to elevate your presence, add dimensions to your ideas, and demonstrate that you're fully present. When you refer to an article or shared document, drop the link in the chat. If you run the meeting, add a link to the agenda in the chat. When others are speaking, respond with support or questions in the chat. Consider the chat window as not just a discussion platform, but a presentational appendage.

Reviewing and practicing these basic principles for virtual and hybrid meetings will make your presence felt no matter where you are.

JOEL SCHWARTZBERG oversees executive communications for a major national nonprofit, is a professional presentation coach, and is the author of *Get to the Point! Sharpen Your Message and Make Your Words Matter* and *The Language of Leadership: How to Engage and Inspire Your Team*. Follow him on LinkedIn and on Twitter @TheJoelTruth.

Adapted from "How to Elevate Your Presence in a Virtual Meeting," on hbr.org, April 8, 2020 (product #H05IOV).

7

Make Time for Small Talk in Your Virtual Meetings

By Bob Frisch and Cary Greene

I t was an unusual confession from a CEO. "During my last staff meeting we must have spent 40% of the time talking about nothing," Jorge said. "We were just hanging out, shooting the breeze, like the old days. It was one of the most enjoyable, productive calls we've had since we shut the office." But afterward, he went on to say, "a few people complained."

On a call shortly after, Rose, the company's president, added her perspective. "I was not happy, and neither was our CFO, so I talked to Jorge about it," she explained. "Maybe he's got time on his hands, but I'm on Zoom 12 hours a day. Frankly, if I've got a half hour available during the day, I'd rather walk out of my home office and spend the time with my husband and kids."

Although tension always exists between time spent on the substance of a meeting and time spent socializing, most recurring meetings reach a natural balancing point—at least until the equilibrium is disrupted by a change in circumstances or in the personalities involved. Having to meet virtually has tipped that balance.

The loss of small talk seems to be a challenge not only for Jorge and Rose but for many executives. We've identified two common causes.

"Gathering time" is gone. Pre-Covid, executives often had the chance to casually chat with colleagues while they grabbed coffee before a meeting started. Once at the table, these one-on-one or small group conversations sometimes continued for a while longer, perhaps spreading to the larger group before the meeting got down to business.

With video calls, as participants' windows pop up on the screen, it's either talk to everyone or don't talk. As a result, video etiquette seems to call for meetings to get underway either on schedule or shortly after the relevant participants have signed on, depending on the culture. But the best opportunity for a team to chat without impinging on meeting time—those few minutes of premeeting gathering time—has vanished.

Zoom fatigue is rampant. Both Jorge and Rose are energized by their jobs and the success their team had in adapting and pivoting through Covid. But like many executives, they're exhausted from the back-to-back, morning-to-night, continuous flow of video calls.

Many managers find themselves depleted of energy before their workday is over. It shouldn't be a surprise that prolonging a call unnecessarily might strike these folks as irritating, especially when they know that the moment they leave the meeting they'll be free to spend time on the other, sorely needed side of the work-life balance.

But making time for small talk is important. Jorge rightly believes that continuing his team's extraordinary level of performance depends on maintaining and growing the culture he's spent the past few years instilling in the company and among his team. Jorge's concerns are centered on creating, maintaining, and deepening individual and group relationships. He knows that quickly integrating new members into the team requires more than a series of background briefings. It involves getting to know the other members as people as well.

Those moments, for Jorge, surface during or after unstructured conversations. There's a virtue to "hanging out." It's the chitchat, the side conversations that lift emotions and promote well-being. It's one way we strengthen and deepen relationships and is critical to building high-performing teams.

How to Reintroduce Small Talk into Your Meetings

While we can't solve the problem of finding a virtual replacement for a round of golf, an afternoon's sail, or a long dinner with a few glasses of wine, we have come up with a few ways to help reinstate this important component of your meetings.

1. Make small talk an agenda item, not an afterthought

Jorge didn't have any plan in place when he allowed a large part of his meeting to devolve into a conversation about nothing. It just happened. And the fact that it was spontaneous, while energizing and enjoyable to Jorge, turned it into an imposition for Rose and others.

Were he to do it again, Jorge might inform the team of his intent to deliberately create space for more personal, informal interactions as part of their virtual meetings. While this may seem paradoxical—planning and scheduling the casual and spontaneous—creating expectations and setting boundaries will increase the team's comfort to embrace the change. (See the sidebar "Fight the Pull of Transactional Relationships" to learn more about purposefully creating virtual hallway encounters.)

2. Start with an individual check-in or icebreaker

An activity or icebreaker at the beginning of a meeting is a timeless way to connect participants. Over the years, groups attending regularly recurring meetings, like Jorge's weekly staff meeting, often abandon icebreakers as unnecessary.

In a virtual world, beginning meetings with an icebreaker is a first step to reintroducing small talk.

FIGHT THE PULL OF TRANSACTIONAL RELATIONSHIPS

Colleagues working together in an office have plenty of organic opportunities to develop a low-key, ambient awareness of each other's lives. From elevator rides to breakroom encounters, it's easy to run into someone, strike up a conversation, and learn everything from where they last vacationed to what their favorite sports teams are. That information isn't essential to performing your job, of course, so it's easy to overlook its importance. But it provides a form of "social glue" that enables you to connect with colleagues beyond the purely transactional format of Zoom calls discussing a particular project or account.

Research has shown that online negotiations are far more likely to be resolved successfully when participants share personal information with one another and thereby create a bond, rather than sticking

(continued)

to "just the facts" of the deal.[1] Similarly, a colleague who feels a personal connection to you is almost certainly more likely to advocate for you when you're not in the room, or volunteer to help you even when it's not convenient, as compared to someone with whom you have a more distant relationship.

As a remote worker, you'll have to think harder about how to engineer these connections; you can't rely on bumping into someone who invites you to lunch. You'll likely have to be the initiator, whether you decide to invite colleagues for one-on-one video chats or host a virtual networking event. But the effort is worth it, given the powerful impact of social connections on both your reputation at work and your ability to do your job successfully.

Dorie Clark is a marketing strategist and keynote speaker who teaches at Duke University's Fuqua School of Business and has been named one of the top 50 business thinkers in the world by Thinkers50. Her latest book is *The Long Game: How to Be a Long-Term Thinker in a Short-Term World* (HBR Press, 2021).

Adapted from "Staying Visible When Your Team Is in the Office . . . But You're WFH," on hbr.org, July 30, 2021 (product #H06GE9).

One client asked each individual to take a minute and share what had been happening in their lives, both professionally and personally. She went first and modeled the tone and candor of the exercise, explaining that a loved one was ill and describing how it had affected her. Others followed suit, and immediately the group felt more connected and comfortable with one another.

Alternatively, inject some fun at the beginning of the meetings. One CEO asked each team member to send along a baby picture of themselves. At the beginning of each meeting, the CEO shares one picture and asks each team member to guess who it is. This often leads to laughter and some good storytelling—pretty good results for an investment of two to four minutes.

3. Introduce agenda items designed around opinions and conjecture

Put your team on a level playing field. Occasionally bring up a discussion topic on which most people will have an opinion, use polling to get your team's individual views on the table, and then let the conversation meander.

Instead of a "conversation about nothing," Jorge should swap in a topic designed to collect opinions on broad themes or focused on creative brainstorming. These are still "talking about the business," but at a much higher altitude than the transactional, day-to-day agenda items. And because they're opinion based by design, it becomes hard for any team member to claim special expertise that overrides the opinions of the others.

A question like "When do you think travel patterns and traffic will return to pre-Covid numbers?" has no right answer. Fifteen minutes discussing the range of views among Jorge's team on this or a comparable topic would make a great start.

4. Leave unstructured time at the end of team meetings

Another way to open up an opportunity for informal chatter while accommodating Rose's concerns for efficiency is simple—leave the choice up to each participant.

If Rose knows in advance that Jorge may choose to use 15–20 minutes of unallocated time at the end of his next staff meeting just to chat as a group, she can decide for herself whether to hang around. Unlike when the open conversation happened at the beginning, Rose will no longer feel ambushed, trapped on the call with no idea how long it will take to get back to business. If she needs to move on, she'll just move on. And Jorge will have an even more convivial group, knowing that everyone around the table knows they too can drift out of the conversation when needed.

Small talk is a big deal. It's time to bring this missing piece of your team's culture to the virtual world.

BOB FRISCH is the founding partner of the Strategic Offsites Group. A regular contributor to *Harvard Business Review* since the seminal "Off-Sites That Work" in 2006, Bob wrote the bestselling *Who's in the Room? How Great Leaders Structure and Manage the Teams Around Them* and coauthored *Simple Sabotage*. He has earned over 10 million frequent flier miles facilitating strategy meetings in 19 countries.

CARY GREENE is the managing partner of the Strategic Offsites Group, a consultancy focused on designing and facilitating strategy conversations for executive teams and boards. He is the coauthor of *Simple Sabotage* and a frequent contributor to HBR, with articles featured across five collections including the *HBR Guides to Making Better Decisions*, *Making Every Meeting Matter*, and *Remote Work*.

Note

1. Don Moore et al., "Long and Short Routes to Success in Electronically Mediated Negotiations: Group Affiliations and Good Vibrations," *Organizational Behavior and Human Decision Processes* 77, no. 1 (January 1999): 22–43, https://doi.org/10.1006/obhd.1998.2814

Adapted from content posted on hbr.org,
February 18, 2021 (product #H067DY).

8

Yes, Virtual Presenting Is Weird

By Sarah Gershman

once worked with a CEO who told me that she dreads giving virtual presentations. "I used to enjoy getting up in front of an audience," she explained. "I loved working the room. Now, I feel like I'm speaking into a black hole."

What is it about virtual presenting that can feel so *unnerving*? Surprisingly, one answer to this question can be found right outside our windows by listening to how birds communicate. Birds call out to one another primarily for survival—to signal danger and to attract a mate.[1] Imagine how scary it must be for a bird to call out and receive no response. This is how we often feel when we present on Zoom—like the bird who calls out and hears only silence.

When we present in person, we rely on the audience response to confirm that our message is being received. In virtual presentations, however, we lack audience feedback. We no longer see body language. We often don't see people nodding their heads (or nodding off if they are bored), and it is much harder to make eye contact. As a result, we feel as if no one is listening. Unfortunately, this makes us even more anxious about speaking. And even worse, because we *feel* as if no one is listening, we *speak* as if no one is listening. We sound less connected to the audience. We speak in more of a monotone. We ramble and have trouble finishing a thought. This only makes the problem worse—it both reinforces our anxiety and makes for a poor presentation. After all, the more disconnected we sound, the harder it is for the audience to listen.

How can we solve this problem? How can we relieve our own anxiety that nobody's listening to our virtual presentations? And more importantly, how can we help the virtual audience feel our presence and hear our message?

The answer is to virtually simulate the call-and-response function we experience during in-person presentations. Like a bird, a virtual speaker must deliberately and compellingly call and elicit a response.

Here are three ways to elicit greater audience response and connection in your virtual presentations.

Use the chat, especially when you start. The hardest part of a virtual presentation is the beginning, when it feels most like nobody is listening. "Uh . . . is this working?" or "Can everyone hear me?" gets the presentation off to a weak start and reinforces the distance. Instead, begin with something that brings everyone in. The chat function is a great way to get immediate audience response. You could begin with a relevant question and ask people to type the answer in the chat. For example, you might ask everyone to write one thing they hope to learn from the presentation. The chat is especially helpful to introverts who may not want to speak up. Make sure to read aloud at least some of the answers (and use first names if you can). When you engage the audience immediately, you feel as though people are listening, which raises your confidence for the rest of the presentation.

Even when the audience can't respond, keep it conversational. Webinars, with their lack of audience response, can make a speaker particularly nervous. One way to simulate the back-and-forth nature of a conversation is to ask rhetorical questions throughout your presentation. For example, when you introduce a new idea, you might say, "Are you ready to try something new?" Or, if you want people to notice something, you might say, "Do you see the shift from low to high on the chart?" For the audience, rhetorical questions create open loops in the brain, which we then want to close by answering them in our heads.[2] This helps the audience stay active and connected to your content, even when they can't talk to you. By continuously asking questions, you'll feel more as though you are having a conversation, which eases some of the anxiety.

Empathize. One of the reasons why giving a virtual presentation can feel so unsettling is that we find it hard to emotionally connect with the audience. By taking a few moments before a presentation to put yourself in the shoes of the listener, you will feel more emotionally connected to them when you speak.[3] Keep in mind that it's difficult and draining to listen to a virtual presentation. What can you do to make it easier? By empathizing with your virtual audience, you shift the focus away from yourself (and what others think of you), which relieves speaking anxiety. Empathizing also helps you design a presentation that best helps your audience and serves their needs.

Virtual presentations are inherently awkward. The lack of audience response, the inability to "read the room," and the lack of direct eye contact all increases our anxiety. Re-creating the back and forth of a conversation—even in a webinar—can help you feel more connected to your audience, which will make you sound less remote and more connected. It's easy to forget that, though you can't see your virtual audience, they really are still there. They are listening, and now more than ever, they need *your* attention.

SARAH GERSHMAN is the president of Green Room Speakers, a communications firm based in Washington, DC. She is a professor at the McDonough School of Business at Georgetown University, where she teaches public speaking to students from around the globe.

Notes

1. Heidi Almond, "How Do Birds Communicate?," *Sciencing*, October 4, 2021, https://sciencing.com/birds-communicate-4567063.html.
2. Chelsea Baldwin, "3 Damn Good, Psychology-Backed Reasons You Need Rhetorical Questions in Your On-Site Copy," *The MVP*, March 7, 2016, https://medium.com/the-mvp/3-damn-good-psychology-backed-reasons-you

-need-rhetorical-questions-in-your-on-site-copy-75e6e855adb6.

3. Elizabeth A. Segal, "Five Ways Empathy Is Good for Your Health," *Psychology Today*, December 17, 2018, https://www.psychologytoday.com/us/blog/social-empathy/201812/five-ways-empathy-is-good-your-health.

Adapted from content posted on hbr.org, November 4, 2020 (product #H05YM3).

9

Five Ways to Reduce Rudeness in the Remote Workplace

By Dana Kabat-Farr and Rémi Labelle-Deraspe

As organizations adopt virtual operations as a core way of conducting business, leaders will need to understand the social implications (both good and bad) of cyber work before adopting it long term. Of particular concern is how diverse teams can come together, forge connections, and collaborate effectively in online environments. Our research on selective incivility—subtle slights, interruptions, and disregard experienced by women, members of racial minorities, and other marginalized employees—demonstrates that incivility is damaging to performance and deteriorates team functioning.[1] Virtual spaces are uniquely susceptible to this form of insidious behavior, as online team meetings, chat rooms, and team management spaces provide ample opportunity for disrespect to thrive. Managers need to be keenly aware of how incivility manifests online in order to create spaces that include all voices and diverse contributions.

Incivility Is Amplified in Virtual Settings

Our research on workplace incivility shows that while most of us experience rudeness at some point, employees of color, LGBTQ+ employees, and those with other marginalized identities experience it more often.[2] Moreover, virtual incivility in particular is a cause for concern for employees of color in the U.S.[3] Being interrupted, spoken over, glossed over, or receiving snide remarks are all examples of incivility.[4] In an online environment, it's even easier to act uncivilly: Physical distance makes us feel separated from one another, and there are few consequences for bad actors.[5] Organizations often brush off these rude experiences as unimportant or, worse yet, consider it "just the ways things are done around here." The crucial problem for a diverse workforce is that these trivialized experiences also translate into poor work and mental health outcomes for those at the receiving end.[6] And when incivility becomes a daily hassle, marginalized members take that as a cue that they're not respected or valued, and they may leave the organization all together.[7]

Incivility is particularly damaging due to its ambiguous nature—that is, it's often unclear whether the person slighting another intends harm.[8] For example, we talked to a health systems employee who recounted an email detailing patient care that ended with "Have you got it?" They read this as questioning their intelligence, while someone else might read it as a clarifying question. The ambiguous nature of incivility leaves room for interpretation. When the cause of the mistreatment is unclear, employees are more likely to make internal attributions ("Was it something I did?" "Do they think I'm not competent?"), leading to self-doubt, lowered self-esteem, and rumination.[9] As a veiled form of bias, this process can be just as damaging—to the employee as well as the organization—as overt forms of discrimination, where attributions are more easily externalized ("He's sexist" or "She's racist"). Subtle forms of discrimination are also harder to identify and address using organizational policies, making them more likely to be a chronic stressor for marginalized employees.[10]

The switch to virtual operations can amplify the concerns of employees who already felt excluded at work. Subtle interpersonal messaging during virtual meetings signals to some that their voices are valued and that they belong and to others that they may be best kept on mute. Casual encounters in the hallways, break rooms, and elevators are less frequent or nonexistent, so virtual meetings may be their only tangible connection to the organization. Targets of incivility are also less able to find social support to cope, making the experience more isolating.

Incivility Flies Under the Radar

Research shows that only 1% to 6% of employees report incivility to managers.[11] To some extent, that makes sense. Formally reporting that someone cut you off in a meeting may seem like overreacting to a small mishap. However, instead of viewing these incivilities as isolated experiences, we should identify patterns of slights and indignities that can reveal the ways in which incivility eats away at the commitment, satisfaction, and performance of members from diverse backgrounds. For example, it isn't just that John cut you off in a meeting yesterday—it's that he did a similar thing in the last meeting, and before that, his boss left you off an important email. Recent studies have found that these hostile exchanges are unpleasant and irritating for employees, leaving them feeling devalued.[12]

If employees don't report incivility, how do they handle it? The most common response is to avoid the instigator. Research suggests that neither avoiding nor confronting the instigator reduces future incidents, leaving targets with few viable options.[13] In the case of selective incivility, confronting instigators may also mean going against established power dynamics and accusing someone of biased treatment. Again, because of the subtle, ambiguous nature of incivility, targets are not likely to take on the risk and discomfort of confrontation when the instigator might accuse them of being oversensitive and a troublemaker.

What Managers Can Do

Organizations are increasingly sinking major financial investments into diversity trainings and implicit bias workshops. While these may be beneficial in educating employees about the fundamental facts of company policies, laws, and psychological processes, research suggests that they do little to create the type of inclusive environments necessary to have a healthy and productive diverse workforce. How connections are forged and maintained in a virtual environment will rely on some intentional efforts by managers.

Leaders can use micro-interventions—everyday words and deeds that counteract, change, or stop subtle discrimination—to create contexts where selective incivility is less likely and that provide an avenue for apology and growth when infractions do occur.[14] Incivility prevention and intervention are crucial in fostering the productive and inclusive teams that many organizations are striving for as they implement their remote or hybrid work plans. Here are our best pieces of advice for conducting virtual work that will cultivate positive relationships among your team.

Make the expectation for respectful interactions explicit. Although leaders often feel as though addressing social norms is superfluous to productivity, we know that time spent ruminating, seeking support, or retaliating following rude interactions is time and money wasted for organizations. Furthermore, Lilia Cortina of the University of Michigan and her colleagues detail the human costs of incivility: physiological damage including impaired memory, increased cardiovascular activity, and disruption of insulin production.[15] All of this adds up to more sick leave, increased mental health concerns, and negative spillover into family relationships.

One way to make the team's expectations for respect explicit is to jointly create a team contract that includes respect as a core principle. Examples include, "We will not speak over one another in meetings," or "Contributions will be recorded via the team chat to ensure all members get credit for their ideas." Limiting the use of smartphones for multitasking and implementing more structured protocols for meetings with built-in opportunities to connect and collaborate may also be important principles to enhance respect in your workplace. By setting a clear standard of respect and norms around constructive dialogue and conflict, leaders and team members have a starting point when addressing patterns of low-level disrespect and disregard.

Make following up on interpersonal mishaps a norm. All too often, we hear from employees who are trying to make sense of a recent Zoom mishap. *Did he mean to cut me off? Why do my contributions get swallowed up without people noticing? No one seems to even notice when I log on or off.* In the virtual workplace, employees have less time to debrief or get social support from colleagues following ambiguous mishaps like these.[16] By acknowledging the importance of small interpersonal gestures, teams can create a norm where members can follow up on things that they perceived as a slight.[17]

Video meetings open the door for misinterpretation, as virtual interactions are less rich than in-person ones.[18] For example, when brainstorming as a team recently, one of us became lost in thought and had a prolonged and awkward stare into the webcam. Face-to-face, it would have been easier to decipher this as contemplation rather than distraction or boredom.

Make it less awkward to inquire about such "lost in translation" experiences to reduce ambiguity for others. One way to start this process is to be open about your own potential missteps. Follow up immediately by acknowledging that you sensed awkwardness or that you weren't sure your message was conveyed appropriately. As a leader, you set the example for not rushing past these moments and pausing to ensure the message was correctly received.

Call people in. Calling people *out* alienates individuals and fosters a sense of fear and social derision that can permeate your organizational culture. Instead, if you'd like to correct a behavior that was perceived as rude, call people *in* to have a conversation with the goal of changed behavior. This is based on the work of Loretta Ross, who advocates for addressing interpersonal missteps by opening the door to conversation, understanding, and learning. By addressing hurtful behavior through private, respectful conversation with the instigator, you leave the door open to collaboration. Calling instigators in should be paired with extending support to the person who was treated disrespectfully as a way of closing the loop and signaling that you noticed and addressed the incivility.

When having these conversations, avoid blame and snap judgments; instead, focus on the impact of the behavior and work together to find solutions. People often respond best to similarity and familiarity.[19] By focusing on similarities and shared experiences, we can take steps to create connections and build trust. Finding these points of connection is especially important when working across differences—viewing coworkers as individual people with shared connections helps to erode implicit stereotypes that undergird subtle forms of disrespect.[20] If you yourself are called in for rude behavior, listen with respect and apologize when necessary. As a leader, making a public apology is a powerful way to influence the culture of your workplace.

Beware of bias. Even chronic instigators of incivility may be unaware of the impact of their behavior. Try to avoid thinking of these employees as "bad apples" but rather acknowledge that while most of us think of ourselves as upstanding moral citizens, we are all works in progress. This might help reduce their defensiveness, as the negative associations, stereotypes, and assumptions we hold about others, even implicitly, influence our behaviors and stem from long histories involving racism, sexism, homophobia, and xenophobia. While most of us don't endorse these systems of oppression, it's very difficult to extricate ourselves from them completely, and all too often, our actions are informed by and reinforce them.

Allies or bystanders can also miss the mark for respectful behavior, even if they have positive intentions.[21] We're all on our own journeys to become "goodish people," as Dolly Chugh, author of *The Person You Mean to Be: How Good People Fight Bias*, puts it. By understanding the cultural, societal, and historical complexity around the marginalization of various groups, we can set ourselves on a learning orientation to correct our stumbles and mistakes. As leaders, we can set an example by correcting the subtle ways bias manifests online. For example, research finds that Black women's contributions are not remembered as accurately as those of their peers and are often misattributed to others.[22] Check that your online meetings allow for equal voices and that contributions are tracked.

Don't skip the "niceties." You know those premeeting updates on puppy training, new recipes, and family affairs? Don't rush past them. Our research suggests that taking a personal interest in employees translates into feelings of thriving and empowerment.[23] Instead of viewing this time as irrelevant to productivity, create space and time (even five minutes) for people to share what's going on in their lives. This could be a short activity where everyone contributes, such as sharing one good thing that happened to them that day. This will ensure quiet voices or new members feel welcome and provides an opportunity to foster personal connections.

As organizations adopt virtual operations as a core way of conducting business in the long term, managers need to be conscious of the powerful effect of slights, snubs, and other rude behavior on employee and team functioning. For employees from marginalized groups, patterns of uncivil experiences may signal that they don't belong in the organization or that their perspective is not welcome. Managers can create an antidote to incivility by providing opportunities for personal connections and accountability to shared norms of respect.

DANA KABAT-FARR is an associate professor at the Rowe School of Business of the Dalhousie University. Her research focuses on workplace social experiences—both negative (incivility, harassment) and positive (citizenship). She pays particular attention to gender harassment, incivility as a covert form of discrimination against women and people of color, and positive and negative experiences that influence employees' ability to thrive.

RÉMI LABELLE-DERASPE is a lecturer in organizational behavior at the School of Business of the Université du Québec à Trois-Rivières. His research investigates incivility, harassment, modern forms of discrimination, and violent behaviors, with a focus on interventions to address subtle mistreatment.

Notes

1. Dana Kabat-Farr, Isis H. Settles, and Lilia M. Cortina, "Selective Incivility: An Insidious Form of Discrimination in Organizations," *Equality, Diversity and Inclusion* 39, no. 3 (2020): 253–260, https://doi.org/10.1108/EDI-09 -2019-0239.

2. Ibid.

3. Shanna Daniels and LaDonna M. Thornton, "Race and Workplace Discrimination: The Mediating Role of Cyber Incivility and Interpersonal Incivility," *Equality, Diversity and Inclusion* 39, no. 3 (2020): 319–335, https://doi.org/10.1108/EDI-06-2018-0105.

4. Lilia M. Cortina et al., "Incivility in the Workplace: Incidence and Impact," *Journal of Occupational Health Psychology* 6, no. 1 (2001): 64–80, https://doi.org/10.1037/1076-8998.6.1.64.

5. Gary W. Giumetti et al., "Cyber Incivility @ Work: The New Age of Interpersonal Deviance," *Cyberpsychology, Behavior, and Social Networking* 15, no. 3 (2012): 148–154, https://doi.org/10.1089/cyber.2011.0336.

6. Jingxian Yao et al., "Experienced Incivility in the Workplace: A Meta-analytical Review of Its Construct Validity and Nomological Network," *Journal of Applied Psychology*, April 29, 2021, doi: 10.1037/apl0000870.

7. Nicole T. Buchanan and Isis H. Settles, "Managing (In)visibility and Hypervisibility in the Workplace," *Journal of Vocational Behavior* 113 (2019): 1–5, https://doi.org/10.1016/j.jvb.2018.11.001; Lilia M. Cortina et al., "Selective Incivility as Modern Discrimination in Organizations: Evidence and Impact," *Journal of Management* 39, no. 6 (September 2013): 1579–1605, https://doi.org/10.1177/0149206311418835.

8. Lisa A. Marchiondo, Lilia M. Cortina, and Dana Kabat-Farr, "Attributions and Appraisals of Workplace Incivil-

ity: Finding Light on the Dark Side?," *Applied Psychology* 67 (2018): 369–400, https://doi.org/10.1111/apps.12127.

9. Kristen P. Jones et al., "Not So Subtle: A Meta-Analytic Investigation of the Correlates of Subtle and Overt Discrimination," *Journal of Management* 42, no. 6 (September 2016): 1588–1613, https://doi.org/10.1177/0149206313506466.

10. Ibid.

11. Lilia M. Cortina and Vicki J. Magley, "Patterns and Profiles of Response to Incivility in the Workplace," *Journal of Occupational Health Psychology* 14, no. 3 (2009): 272–288, https://doi.org/10.1037/a0014934.

12. Christine L. Porath and Christine M. Pearson, "Emotional and Behavioral Responses to Incivility," *Journal of Applied Social Psychology* 42, no. S1 (2012): E326–E357, https://doi.org/10.1111/j.1559-1816.2012.01020.x; D. Kabat-Farr, Lilia M. Cortina, and Lisa A. Marchiondo, "The Emotional Aftermath of Incivility: Anger, Guilt, and the Role of Organizational Commitment," *International Journal of Stress Management* 25, no. 2 (2018): 109–128, https://doi.org/10.1037/str0000045.

13. M. Sandy Hershcovis et al., "The Effects of Confrontation and Avoidance Coping in Response to Workplace Incivility," *Journal of Occupational Health Psychology* 23, no. 2 (2018): 163–174, https://doi.org/10.1037/ocp0000078.

14. Derald W. Sue et al., "Disarming Racial Microaggressions: Microintervention Strategies for Targets, White Allies,

and Bystanders," *American Psychologist* 74, no. 1 (2019): 128–142, https://dx.doi.org/10.1037/amp0000296.

15. Lilia M. Cortina, M. Sandy Hershcovis, and Kathryn B. H. Clancy, "The Embodiment of Insult: A Theory of Biobehavioral Response to Workplace Incivility," *Journal of Management*, March 2021, https://doi.org/10.1177/0149206321989798.

16. Gary W. Giumetti et al., "What a Rude E-mail! Examining the Differential Effects of Incivility versus Support on Mood, Energy, Engagement, and Performance in an Online Context," *Journal of Occupational Health Psychology* 18, no. 3 (2013): 297–309, https://doi.org/10.1037/a0032851.

17. Justin Kruger et al., "Egocentrism over E-mail: Can We Communicate as Well as We Think?," *Journal of Personality and Social Psychology* 89, no. 6 (2005): 925–936, doi: 10.1037/0022-3514.89.6.925.

18. Luis L. Martins, Lucy L. Gilson, and M. Travis Maynard, "Virtual Teams: What Do We Know and Where Do We Go from Here?," *Journal of Management* 30, no. 6 (December 2004): 805–835, https://doi.org/10.1016/j.jm.2004.05.002.

19. Donn Erwin Byrne, *The Attraction Paradigm* (Cambridge, MA: Academic Press, 1971).

20. Lisa Nishii, Creating Gender-Inclusive Climates and Conversations," in *Creating Gender-Inclusive Organizations: Lessons from Research and Practice*, Ellen Ernst Kossek and Kyung Hee Lee, eds. (Toronto:

University of Toronto Press, 2020), 15–52, https://doi.org/10.3138/9781487518608-004 .

21. Shannon K. Cheng et al., "Helping or Hurting?: Understanding Women's Perceptions of Male Allies," *Personnel Assessment and Decisions* 5, no. 2 (2019), https://doi.org/10.25035/pad.2019.02.006.

22. Amanda K. Sesko and Monica Biernat, "Prototypes of Race and Gender: The Invisibility of Black Women," *Journal of Experimental Social Psychology* 46, no. 2 (2010): 356–360, https://doi.org/10.1016/j.jesp.2009.10.016.

23. Dana Kabat-Farr and Lilia M. Cortina, "Receipt of Interpersonal Citizenship: Fostering Agentic Emotion, Cognition, and Action in Organizations," *Journal of Applied Social Psychology* 47 (2017): 74–89, https://doi.org/10.1111/jasp.12421.

Adapted from content posted on hbr.org,
August 19, 2021 (product #H06ITI).

10

Stay Mindful When You're Working Remotely

By Alyson Meister and Amanda Sinclair

t's no surprise that online work is depleting our energy and resilience. The evidence shows that many of us are working longer hours, suffering chronic stress, and burning out at levels the world has never witnessed. At the same time, we're longing for and losing our social connections and sometimes experiencing profound loneliness and grief in solitude. To regain energy, find renewed pleasure in our work, and truly connect with colleagues and friends, we need to find ways to block out the noise in our virtual reality.

One way we can do that is through cultivating mindfulness—online.

Mindfulness is the choice we make to be present in the here and now: this moment, in this meeting, with this person or group of people. Research shows that most activities of our working lives, from working on an independent task to team meetings and one-on-ones, benefit from being conducted with mindfulness. By pausing, checking in with others, or starting meetings with a few moments of meditation or reflection, our stress levels drop and we feel more connected to our purpose and to others in the room. We listen better and feel happier.

But how can we be mindful in an online working world? How can we be truly present for others when we couldn't be (physically) farther from one another?

What we learned from the pandemic is that online and remote working doesn't have to be a barrier to our capacity to deliver leadership presence, empathize and connect with colleagues, and build strong workplace communities. Contrary to popular misconceptions, you don't have to retreat to a mountain top or a meditation cushion to practice mindfulness. You can do it while working from home by:

- Pausing and noticing where your thinking mind is

- Purposefully bringing your awareness to the people and context that are with you virtually

- Suspending your own narratives, agendas, judgments, and ego to offer your full online presence, evidenced through eye contact, warm and responsive facial expressions, and minimized multitasking

You can apply these three principles of mindfulness to managing and leading online.

From doing to being: Offer your presence. Action is the hallmark of managers. It's what they're noticed for and measured on: doing, achieving, producing, organizing, controlling. Remote and hybrid working environments have thrust managers into excessive patterns of "doing." But sometimes, who and how you're *being* can be more important than your actions.

To cultivate trust and motivate and inspire others, pay attention to how you're being with them. Are you rushed or distracted? Is your mind on the next meeting or your to-do list? To enhance the quality of your leadership presence with others, take a moment to reflect on your physical and emotional state when entering a new meeting. Through your virtual presence, what energy will you convey to this set of colleagues or clients? Will you bring the tough conversation you just had with someone else into this new one? Will you offer a sense of calm and reassurance?

Another's presence (or lack thereof) is noticeable. When someone is speaking, are you using the moment to check your email, send a text, or schedule a meeting? You may think that none of this shows in online working contexts. But just as in a face-to-face meeting room, virtual participants know whether and how you're truly present with them—emotions and attention can be broadcast, felt, and contagious across virtual boundaries. Even in a big online town hall, the audience can sense if the speaker is truly with them, and the speaker knows if most of the audience is elsewhere.

Lead by example when working remotely. Try to have your camera on and ask others to do so if possible. Ensure others can feel your presence by establishing eye contact, and use your body and posture to convey interest and empathy. If you know you just can't help but look, turn off those enticing email notifications.

Shifting your focus to how you're being doesn't mean that things don't get done. And none of these shifts in your awareness and attention take more than a few moments. But they do have an impact on you and on those you're working with.

From future to present: Be here, now. Managers are taught to relentlessly plan for the future. Yet always having your mind on next month's targets or next year's profits can mean you miss life today. You forgo important opportunities for connection and empowering others if you're in your mind, planning "the next step" or worrying about something that might not happen.

Take a moment to step back from the busyness and view your tasks with perspective—looking down from the balcony. What or who is important right now? Ask yourself: Am I postponing life, thinking that all the good stuff will come next month, next year, or when some milestone or key event happens? Postponing life can exacerbate unhappiness and stress. We hold out for when things will improve but don't see all the beautiful small things around us now: a fun meal with family, a morning walk or run, the sharing of a special moment, or a celebration with colleagues.

Next time you're in a virtual meeting and notice your mind has wandered off, catch yourself. Bring your mind to where your body *actually* is—this present moment, right here, right now. Take a few seconds to anchor your awareness in the now by drawing on your senses. Look outside if you can and take in any sky or green that may be visible. Relax your shoulders and your jaw. Breathe out. These momentary connections with your physical senses are the gateways to being more present. Sharing some words of gratitude for people showing up and for what exists in the here and now can help others to pause and pay attention. They may notice they've been ruminating and can choose to tune in, not tune out. Practicing mindfulness techniques like these has been demonstrated to lift moods, foster well-being, and improve overall psychological health.

From me to you: Enabling connection and community. When people are talking, where is *your* mind? Is it with them? Or are you waiting for a gap to jump in with your opinion or experience? Can you suspend your own agendas and ego needs to hear what people on the team need? Try deepening your listening. Try listening without wanting to "fix" people or (perhaps silently) insisting they get over things. Deep listening is generous. Encourage the person speaking to discover and voice a way forward. They will appreciate and be empowered by it, finding their own path or solution.

In our executive development work, we have found that virtual meetings can reduce barriers for people to speak and to have their voice and presence heard and felt. For example, tools like "raise hand" indicators and simultaneous chat functions enable different ways for people to offer insight and signal their contribution. Further, that everyone has one equal-sized window with only a headshot in a virtual meeting can diminish stereotypes, hierarchies, and power differentials as certain physical and status markers are removed. As a mindful leader, be aware of who is present and pay particular attention to inclusion. Welcome and seek people's input, especially from those who usually don't say much.

Endorsing expressions of openness and vulnerability can help cultivate a culture of appreciation and psychological safety. As a leader, you might offer some vulnerability about where you are right now, which will open the space for others to express how they really are. You might be juggling the needs of a sick child or a parent in aged care. The circumstances of online working have meant we've had to get more real, with people tuning in from their living rooms and bedrooms. Our colleagues have families, pets, and other competing needs to accommodate. We've had to take off our office masks, our makeup, and our constructed work identities and allow others to see us more fully. This has surely been a good thing.

ALYSON MEISTER is a professor of leadership and organizational behavior at IMD Business School in Lausanne, Switzerland. Follow her on Twitter @alymeister.

AMANDA SINCLAIR is an author, researcher, and teacher in leadership, change, gender, and diversity. A professorial fellow at Melbourne Business School, her books include *Leadership for the Disillusioned*, *Leading Mindfully*, and, with Christine Nixon, *Women Leading*. Amanda is also a yoga and meditation teacher, and much of her teaching and coaching focuses on introducing insights and practices from mindfulness to leading well.

Adapted from "Staying Mindful When You're Working Remotely," on hbr.org, March 16, 2021 (product #H068HK).

Index

Contents

Contents

Contents

Contents

Contents

Contents

Contents

How to be human at work.

HBR's Emotional Intelligence Series features smart, essential reading on the human side of professional life from the pages of *Harvard Business Review*. Each book in the series offers uplifting stories, practical advice, and research from leading experts on how to tend to our emotional well-being at work.

Harvard Business Review Emotional Intelligence Series

Available in paperback or ebook format. The specially priced six-volume set includes:

- Mindfulness
- Resilience
- Influence and Persuasion
- Authentic Leadership
- Happiness
- Empathy

HBR.ORG

Buy for your team, clients, or event.
Visit hbr.org/bulksales for quantity discount rates.

Engage with HBR content the way you want, on any device.

With HBR's subscription plans, you can access world-renowned case studies from Harvard Business School and receive four **free eBooks**. Download and customize prebuilt **slide decks and graphics** from our **Data & Visuals** collection. With HBR's archive, top 50 best-selling articles, and five new articles every day, HBR is more than just a magazine.

Subscribe Today
HBR.org/success

The most important management ideas all in one place.

We hope you enjoyed this book from *Harvard Business Review*. For the best ideas HBR has to offer turn to HBR's 10 Must Reads Boxed Set. From books on leadership and strategy to managing yourself and others, this 6-book collection delivers articles on the most essential business topics to help you succeed.

HBR's 10 Must Reads Series

The definitive collection of ideas and best practices on our most sought-after topics from the best minds in business.

- Change Management
- Collaboration
- Communication
- Emotional Intelligence
- Innovation
- Leadership
- Making Smart Decisions

- Managing Across Cultures
- Managing People
- Managing Yourself
- Strategic Marketing
- Strategy
- Teams
- The Essentials

hbr.org/mustreads

Buy for your team, clients, or event.
Visit hbr.org/bulksales for quantity discount rates.

Harvard
Business
Review
Press